KATY PERRY

BIOGRAPHY

Teenage Dream to Pop Queen

(Inspirational Book For Kids)

Eunice A. John

Katy Perry biography

TABLE OF CONTENTS

Katy Perry biography

Katy Perry biography

CHAPTER 8: CHALLENGES AND TRIUMPHS

8.1 How Katy Perry Stayed True to Herself

CHAPTER 9: JUDGE ON AMERICAN IDOL

9.1 Bringing Fun and Kindness to the Show

CHAPTER 10: PERSONAL LIFE

10.1 Katy Perry as a Mom and Partner

CHAPTER 11: LEGACY

CONCLUSION

INTRODUCTION

Have you ever had a big dream? One so bright and bold that it lit up your whole heart? Katy Perry did—and she chased it with everything she had.

This is the story of a girl named Katheryn, who grew up singing in church, writing songs in her bedroom, and believing in the power of music.

Even when things got tough—and they did—she never gave up on the dream inside her. She believed she could shine, even when the world told her she couldn't.

Katy Perry didn't become a superstar overnight. She faced rejection, doubt, and heartbreak. But she turned her struggles into songs, her fears into strength, and her dreams into reality.

With sparkly costumes, colorful hair, and a voice that made millions sing along, she became more than just a pop star—she became a symbol of confidence, creativity, and courage.

This book will take you on a journey from Katy's early days to her biggest hits. Along the way, you'll discover how believing in yourself, working hard, and staying true to who you are can turn your own dreams into something amazing.

So get ready to be inspired, because Katy's story isn't just about music—it's about finding your voice and sharing it with the world.

CHAPTER 1: A POP STAR IS BORN

Katy Perry's story begins in a small town in California, where she was born as Katheryn Elizabeth Hudson on October 25, 1984. From a young age, Katy was surrounded by music.

Her parents were both pastors, and the church was a big part of her childhood. It was there that Katy first discovered her love for singing, performing in church choirs, and learning to express herself through music.

But Katy's dreams went far beyond the church walls. She knew she was destined for something bigger. As a teenager, she moved to Nashville, Tennessee, hoping to make it as a country music star. However, Katy soon realized that her true calling was in pop music. She was determined to find her unique sound, and that's exactly what she did.

After years of hard work and a few bumps along the way, Katy signed her first record deal and began recording music that would change her life. Her breakout hit, "I Kissed a Girl," became a massive success and quickly made her a household name. With her bold, colorful style and catchy tunes, Katy Perry became a pop sensation—just like she'd always dreamed.

But Katy's journey didn't stop there. She continued to rise to the top, creating hit after hit and becoming a voice for those who wanted to be themselves, no matter what. With her unforgettable music, larger-than-life personality, and inspiring story, Katy Perry truly became a pop star for the ages.

And the best part? Katy's journey is still unfolding, with more music, more creativity, and more colorful adventures to come. So, what's next for this unstoppable pop star? Only time will tell—but one thing's for sure: Katy Perry is here to stay.

1.1 Who Is Katy Perry

Katy Perry is a famous American singer, songwriter, and pop star known for her catchy songs, vibrant personality, and colorful style. She was born on October 25, 1984, in Santa Barbara, California, as Katheryn Elizabeth Hudson. Katy first became interested in music at a young age and started singing in church choirs. Her early love for music led her to pursue a career in the entertainment industry.

Katy's breakthrough moment came with her hit single "I Kissed a Girl" in 2008, which quickly made her a pop sensation. Since then, she has released numerous chart-topping songs like "Firework," "Roar," and "Teenage Dream." With her fun, bold, and sometimes quirky image, Katy has become one of the most recognizable pop stars in the world.

In addition to her music career, Katy Perry is known for her larger-than-life personality, eye-catching fashion choices, and her ability to inspire fans to be themselves and follow their dreams. She's also an advocate for charity and social causes, using her platform to make a positive impact in the world.

Katy Perry's success in music, her unique style, and her determination to always be true to herself have made her a role model for many young people. She is often referred to as the "Queen of Colorful Pop" for her fun, energetic approach to music and her vibrant presence in pop culture.

1.2 Early Years in Santa Barbara

Katy Perry was born Katheryn Elizabeth Hudson on October 25, 1984, in the beautiful coastal city of Santa Barbara, California. Growing up in a religious household, Katy's parents were both pastors, and her childhood was shaped by the church.

She spent a lot of her early years moving from one small town to another, following her parents' work as ministers. Because of this, Katy's family didn't have much money, but they always valued faith and hard work.

From a young age, Katy showed a deep love for music. She was surrounded by gospel music, and by the age of nine, she was already singing in church choirs. Her powerful voice caught the attention of many, and it wasn't long before her love for music began to grow into a dream of becoming a professional singer.

Katy's family didn't always support her dream of becoming a pop star. They were focused on their religious beliefs, and they didn't fully understand her desire to pursue music outside the church. Despite this, Katy was determined. At 13, she began taking vocal lessons, and soon after, she was writing her own songs.

As a teenager, Katy moved to the nearby city of Los Angeles to chase her dream of becoming a successful singer. It wasn't an effortless journey, though. She faced many challenges along the way, including struggling to find a record deal and figuring out her own unique style.

But no matter how difficult things got, Katy never gave up on her dream. Though humble, her early years in Santa Barbara laid the groundwork for her amazing journey.

1.3 Discovering Music at a Young Age

Katy Perry's love for music began long before she became a global pop sensation. Growing up in a religious household, her early exposure to music came from singing in church.

Her parents, both pastors, encouraged her to sing gospel songs in church choirs, and it was there that Katy first discovered the power of music to connect with others. As a child, she was captivated by the way music could make people feel happy, inspired, and even moved to tears.

Katy Perry biography

Katy's parents weren't the only ones who noticed her talent. Her voice was strong, powerful, and full of emotion, even as a young girl. By the age of 9, Katy was already performing in church, gaining confidence with each song she sang.

She quickly realized that music was not just something she loved—it was something she wanted to do for the rest of her life.

When Katy was 13, she took a big step toward her dream by taking formal vocal lessons. Her voice grew even stronger, and she began to develop a unique style. But while her early influences were rooted in gospel music, Katy's musical tastes soon began to expand.

She began listening to pop and rock artists, like Alanis Morissette and the Spice Girls, and she found herself drawn to their bold, fun, and rebellious sounds. Katy realized that her true passion was in pop music, and she started writing her own songs, experimenting with different sounds and lyrics.

Her love for music continued to grow throughout her teenage years, and she began performing at local venues in Santa Barbara. Though she faced challenges along the way, Katy never let anything stop her from pursuing her dreams.

Music was her way of expressing herself, and no matter what, she knew she was meant to share her voice with the world.

By the time Katy moved to Los Angeles as a teenager, she was fully committed to making her dreams of becoming a pop star come true. And though she was just beginning her journey, the love for music that she discovered at such a young age would continue to guide her every step of the way.

CHAPTER 2: SCHOOL LIFE

Katy Perry's school years were a bit different from most kids'. Growing up in a religious household, she attended several different schools throughout her childhood, as her family moved from town to town due to her parents' work as pastors. These moves made it challenging for Katy to form long-lasting friendships, but they also gave her a unique perspective on life.

During her early school years, Katy was known for being shy and quiet, especially in the classroom. She was more focused on singing and music than on academics. At a young age, Katy discovered that she had a natural talent for singing and loved performing, especially in church choirs. Though she was a bit reserved at school, music allowed her to express herself in ways words couldn't.

However, Katy's passion for music didn't always fit in with her school life. Her parents were very strict and wanted Katy to focus on her faith and religious studies, so she wasn't allowed to listen to secular music or watch TV shows that weren't related to church teachings. This meant that Katy didn't have access to popular music, but it didn't stop her from discovering it on her own.

She would sneak out and listen to pop music on the radio, and she found herself drawn to the catchy tunes and bold styles of artists like Alanis Morissette and the Spice Girls. These artists, with their fun and rebellious music, inspired Katy to pursue her own dreams of becoming a pop star.

When Katy was old enough to attend high school, she continued to be focused on music. Although she wasn't very interested in traditional school subjects, she poured her energy into learning how to sing and play instruments. At 13, she began taking vocal lessons, and by the time she was 15, she had started writing her own songs.

Her school years may not have been filled with typical teenage experiences, but they were filled with music and a strong sense of purpose. Katy's school life laid the foundation for her future as a singer, and her determination to follow her dreams grew stronger every day.

Despite her struggles fitting in at school, Katy's love for music became her guiding light. She used the experiences of her school years to fuel her creativity, and this passion eventually led her to pursue a career in music.

Katy's school life wasn't easy, but it was filled with moments that helped her become the artist she is today.

2.1 Hardly School And Talent

Katy Perry's school years were a mix of challenges and discovery, especially when it came to balancing her academic life with her growing passion for music. As the daughter of strict religious parents, she attended several different schools, often moving with her family from place to place.

This constant change made it challenging for her to settle in or form deep friendships, which at times left her feeling isolated.

In school, Katy wasn't the loudest or most outgoing student. Instead, she focused on her music, which became her true passion. She wasn't particularly interested in traditional subjects like math or science; her heart was always in the arts.

This didn't go unnoticed by her teachers, who recognized her strong voice and love for performing. Though she was quiet in class, Katy would light up whenever she had the chance to sing.

At a young age, Katy realized that her talent for singing was something special. She started performing in church choirs, where her powerful voice caught the attention of others. Her musical talent was clear, and she began taking it more seriously.

By the time she was 13, Katy was taking vocal lessons, and her talent blossomed even further. Her focus on music deepened as she began writing her own songs, even though she hadn't yet figured out exactly where her talents would take her.

Though her academic life wasn't where she excelled, Katy's musical talent became her true strength. By the time she reached high school, her passion for music was undeniable.

Despite being restricted by her parents' rules and not being able to listen to pop music at home, Katy found ways to explore the music world on her own. She would sneak and listen to popular songs and began experimenting with different styles, which shaped her own distinctive sound later on.

Katy's early school life and musical talents didn't always seem to match up with her academic environment, but they were building blocks for her future career. Despite not excelling in traditional school subjects, her raw musical talent and determination set her apart and laid the foundation for the pop star she would eventually become.

Through hard work and self-belief, Katy turned her love for music into a career, showing that talent doesn't always fit into the mold of a typical school experience.

CHAPTER 3: THE JOURNEY TO FIND HER SOUND

After moving to Los Angeles at the age of 17, Katy Perry faced the tough reality of trying to break into the music industry. She was determined to become a successful singer, but the road ahead wasn't easy.

She faced rejection after rejection, and it wasn't clear which direction her career would take. Katy tried to fit into many different genres of music, but nothing felt quite right.

At first, Katy recorded Christian music, which was influenced by her upbringing in the church. She even released a gospel album under her real name, Katheryn Hudson, when she was 15.

Unfortunately, the album didn't get the attention she had hoped for, and Katy realized that this wasn't the sound that truly represented her. She felt that there was something bigger waiting for her, but she hadn't found it yet.

Determined to find her true voice, Katy experimented with different musical styles, blending pop, rock, and even a bit of electronic music.

She faced many ups and downs, from signing and leaving record labels to struggling to get her music noticed. But throughout all the challenges, Katy stayed focused on finding the sound that felt authentic to who she was.

Then, in 2007, Katy signed with Capitol Records, and everything began to fall into place. She worked with top producers and songwriters who helped her create the pop sound she had been searching for.

It was with the release of her single "I Kissed a Girl" in 2008 that Katy truly found her musical identity. The song was bold, catchy, and fun—everything that Katy had always wanted her music to be. It became a worldwide hit, and suddenly, Katy Perry was a star.

Her album *One of the Boys* followed, featuring more of her playful and rebellious pop songs, like "Hot n Cold" and "Waking Up in Vegas." This new sound was bold, colorful, and completely Katy Perry. She had finally found her unique style—one that was unapologetic, full of energy, and a true reflection of her fun-loving personality.

Katy's journey to find her sound was full of twists and turns, but it was through each of those experiences that she learned who she truly was as an artist.

The road wasn't easy, but by staying true to herself and experimenting with new ideas, Katy Perry became the pop superstar she is today. And through her music, she continues to inspire others to follow their own dreams and never stop searching for their true selves.

3.1 A Dream And A Guitar

From a young age, Katy Perry had one big dream: to be a successful singer and performer. She wasn't going to let anything stand in her way—not even the challenges of growing up in a religious household where her passion for music was sometimes met with resistance.

What Katy did have was a deep love for singing and a determination to follow her dreams, no matter how tough the journey would be.

At 13, Katy's parents gave her a gift that would change her life forever: a guitar. It was a simple acoustic guitar, but to Katy, it was like holding the key to her future. She spent hours each day teaching herself how to play, using the guitar as a tool to express her thoughts, dreams, and feelings through music.

With the guitar in hand, Katy began writing her own songs—songs about love, life, and the challenges she faced growing up. It wasn't long before music became her escape, her way to connect with the world and herself.

When Katy moved to Los Angeles at 17 to chase her dreams, she took her guitar with her. The city was full of opportunities, but it was also filled with competition. She knew the path would be difficult, but Katy didn't give up. Instead of focusing on the obstacles, she poured her heart into writing songs and playing her guitar.

Katy spent countless hours performing at local clubs and small venues, always striving to improve her music. She wrote songs that reflected her personality—fun, bold, and unique.

But despite her best efforts, she faced rejection after rejection. It wasn't easy to get noticed in the competitive music industry, and she often felt frustrated. Yet, with every setback, she kept playing her guitar, knowing that if she kept trying, her time would come.

Eventually, Katy's persistence paid off. She found her breakthrough with the song "I Kissed a Girl," which became a huge hit in 2008. Her guitar, combined with her creativity, became the foundation of her new pop sound—a sound that was colorful, fresh, and full of energy.

Katy Perry's journey to stardom may have been long and difficult, but it all started with a dream and a guitar.

The guitar became more than just an instrument—it was her voice, her companion, and the tool that helped her share her story with the world. Through her music, Katy has shown that with passion, perseverance, and a little bit of creativity, anything is possible.

3.2 Struggles Before The Spotlight

Before Katy Perry became a global pop superstar, she faced years of struggle and rejection. Her journey to success wasn't easy, and for a long time, it seemed like her dreams might never come true.

But it was during these tough times that Katy learned some of the most important lessons of her life: persistence, self-belief, and never giving up.

When Katy first moved to Los Angeles at the age of 17, she had big dreams of becoming a famous singer. However, the city wasn't as welcoming as she had hoped.

She faced rejection after rejection from record labels and producers who didn't believe in her potential. Katy tried out for several different music styles—country, gospel, even rock—but nothing seemed to click.

She was constantly told that she wasn't what the industry was looking for, and she had to keep moving forward even when things seemed hopeless.

During these years, Katy struggled financially, often living in tiny apartments and struggling to make ends meet. At times, she questioned whether it was worth continuing to chase her dream. But despite the setbacks,

Katy kept working hard. She took odd jobs to pay the bills and spent every spare moment writing songs, performing in small clubs, and honing her skills as an artist.

Katy's early experiences taught her how to be tough and persistent. One of her first major setbacks came when she signed a record deal at the age of 15 and released a gospel album under her real name, Katheryn Hudson.

Unfortunately, the album didn't sell well, and Katy found herself back at square one. She was disappointed but refused to give up on music. Instead of seeing the failure as the end of her story, Katy saw it as a chance to reinvent herself.

She eventually switched from gospel music to pop music, and while this felt like a fresh start, it wasn't easy. The industry was still rejecting her, and it seemed like she just couldn't catch a break. But Katy was determined.

She spent years trying different sounds, finding the right team of producers, and developing her unique pop style. Her breakthrough came with the release of "I Kissed a Girl" in 2008, a bold song that captured her fun, rebellious, and colorful personality. It was the moment her hard work began to pay off.

The struggles before the spotlight were difficult, but they shaped Katy into the artist she is today. She learned that success doesn't come overnight and that every setback was just another step toward achieving her dreams.

Katy's story proves that even when it feels like everything is falling apart, persistence and passion can lead you to greatness.

CHAPTER 4: THE RISE OF KATY PERRY

Katy Perry's rise to stardom didn't happen overnight, but it was a journey fueled by passion, persistence, and a relentless belief in her dreams. After years of struggles, setbacks, and hard work, Katy's big break came in 2008 with the release of her hit single "I Kissed a Girl."

This song quickly shot to the top of the charts, making Katy Perry a household name and propelling her into the spotlight. But her success didn't come easily—it was the result of years of determination and finding her true voice as an artist.

Before "I Kissed a Girl," Katy had already spent years trying to make a name for herself in the music industry. She had moved to Los Angeles as a teenager, facing rejection from record labels and trying out different styles of music.

She initially recorded a gospel album under her birth name, Katheryn Hudson, but it didn't make much of an impact. Katy knew she needed to reinvent herself, so she decided to dive into pop music, experimenting with a fun, bold, and colorful sound that was uniquely hers.

When she signed with Capitol Records, Katy began working with top producers and songwriters to create her breakthrough album, "One of the Boys."

The album was a perfect mix of pop, rock, and catchy melodies, and it showcased Katy's playful, rebellious personality. "I Kissed a Girl" became an instant hit, and it wasn't long before Katy became one of the most talked-about pop stars in the world.

The song's catchy chorus, bold lyrics, and Katy's distinctive style caught the attention of millions, and the song's success catapulted her into global stardom.

Following the success of "I Kissed a Girl," Katy released several more hits, including "Hot n Cold" and "Waking Up in Vegas." Her colorful, fun, and often daring persona made her stand out in the pop world, and fans loved her authenticity and boldness. She had finally found her place in the music industry, and her popularity continued to grow.

But Katy's rise wasn't just about catchy songs—it was about her ability to connect with her audience. She became known for her positive messages of self-expression and individuality, encouraging her fans to be themselves no matter what.

Her anthems, like "Firework" and "Roar," became anthems of empowerment, and she quickly gained a massive following of fans who admired her authenticity and passion.

The rise of Katy Perry is a story of resilience, creativity, and staying true to oneself. From humble beginnings and years of rejection to becoming one of the biggest pop stars in the world, Katy's journey shows that with determination and a willingness to follow your heart, dreams really can come true.

4.1 Teenage Dream" Takes Over the World

In 2010, Katy Perry released *Teenage Dream,* an album that would become a defining moment in her career. The album was packed with unforgettable hits, including "California Gurls," "Teenage Dream," "Firework," and "E.T." Each song became a massive chart-topping success, helping Katy solidify her place as one of the biggest pop stars of her time. *Teenage Dream* was a fresh, energetic collection of songs that captured the feelings of youth, love, and freedom, resonating with fans around the world.

With *Teenage Dream,* Katy not only achieved success but also made history. The album produced five number-one singles on the Billboard Hot 100, a record for a female artist at the time. "Firework" became an anthem of empowerment, inspiring millions to embrace their uniqueness.

Meanwhile, the title tracks "Teenage Dream" and "California Gurls"* became pop anthems for a generation, filled with summer vibes and carefree energy. Katy's rise was unstoppable as she dominated the airwaves and became an international superstar.

Building a colorful brand:

As Katy's music gained worldwide success, she also built a brand that was uniquely her own—bold, colorful, and larger-than-life. Known for her fun, quirky fashion choices and her bright, playful image, Katy Perry turned herself into a pop culture icon.

She embraced vibrant, eye-catching outfits, often incorporating candy-colored wigs, costumes, and themes of fantasy into her music videos and performances. Her sense of style became a visual representation of her music—fun, energetic, and full of personality.

Katy also took her colorful brand beyond music. She became involved in various projects, from launching fragrance lines to appearing in movies like *The Smurfs,* where she voiced the character Smurfette.

Her social media presence, including Twitter and Instagram, also played a major role in connecting her with fans, giving her a platform to showcase her creativity, humor, and genuine connection to her audience.

This colorful, fun, and unapologetically bold brand became a key factor in Katy's success. It set her apart from other artists, and fans loved her for being so true to herself.

Whether she was performing on stage, posting a humorous selfie, or creating an elaborate music video, Katy's brand was one of self-expression, freedom, and individuality.

The Power of Fun and Freedom in Music:

One of the things that sets Katy Perry apart from other artists is her ability to bring a sense of fun and freedom to her music. Her songs, from *"I Kissed a Girl"* to *"Roar,"* are filled with an upbeat energy that encourages listeners to have fun, take risks, and embrace who they truly are.

Katy's music is not just about catchy tunes—it's about freedom of expression and breaking free from the rules.

In a world where music could sometimes be serious or sad, Katy's songs were like a burst of joy and optimism. She created an environment where listeners could dance, sing along, and feel empowered by the positive messages in her lyrics.

Through hits like "Firework," Katy taught her fans to embrace their inner light and let go of insecurities. "Roar" became a global anthem for self-confidence and standing up for oneself, and "Teenage Dream"* celebrated the carefree and adventurous spirit of youth.

Katy's ability to combine fun and freedom with meaningful messages made her music resonate with people of all ages. She gave her fans permission to be themselves, to have fun, and to enjoy life to the fullest.

Through her colorful music and larger-than-life persona, Katy Perry became a symbol of joy, freedom, and living authentically—a message that continues to inspire fans around the world.

CHAPTER 5: BOLD FASHION

Katy Perry's fashion choices have always been as bold and unforgettable as her music. From her early days as a pop star to her global fame, Katy has used her style to express her unique personality and creativity.

Her fashion is a true reflection of her fun-loving, colorful, and fearless approach to life. She's known for wearing daring, playful, and sometimes outrageous outfits that push the boundaries of what's considered normal in the fashion world.

One of the most iconic aspects of Katy's fashion is her love for bright, vibrant colors. She's often seen in candy-colored dresses, eye-catching wigs, and fantastical costumes that look like something out of a dream.

Whether it's a dress made of cupcakes, a bright blue wig, or a playful take on pop culture references, Katy is never afraid to stand out and make a statement with her style.

Her fashion is also a celebration of fun, creativity, and self-expression. Whether performing on stage or attending events, Katy has worn everything from whimsical costumes inspired by desserts and animals to glamorous, high-fashion gowns.

Each outfit tells a story and brings her music to life, adding an extra layer of excitement to her performances. For example, at the 2011 Grammys, Katy wore a floral corset that matched the theme of her hit song "Teenage Dream,"* showing how her style and music are intertwined.

But Katy's bold fashion choices are not just about being eye-catching—they're about owning who she is. She embraces fashion as a way to express her personality and show the world that it's okay to be different.

From quirky accessories to avant-garde gowns, Katy's style encourages her fans to embrace their own individuality and have fun with fashion. Whether she's rocking a leopard print outfit or dressing as a giant strawberry, Katy proves that fashion doesn't have to be serious to make a lasting impression—it just has to be fun.

Her bold fashion has earned her a spot in the fashion world, making her a style icon known for her fearless choices and creativity. Katy's outfits are never just clothes—they're an extension of her playful, larger-than-life persona, and they inspire others to think outside the box and express themselves freely.

5.1 How Fashion Became Part of Her Story

For Katy Perry, fashion has always been more than just clothes—it's an essential part of her identity and creative expression. From the very beginning of her career, Katy understood that the way she presented herself visually could tell as much of a story as the music she created.

Her bold and whimsical fashion choices became a central part of her image, helping her stand out in the crowded pop music world and build a unique persona that was both fun and relatable.

Early on, Katy's style was influenced by her colorful personality and love for self-expression. As a young artist trying to break into the music industry, she realized that standing out visually was just as important as standing out with her voice. She didn't want to just blend in—she wanted her fashion to make a statement.

That's why she often experimented with quirky, eye-catching outfits, from candy-colored wigs to playful costumes, each of which reflected her vibrant, carefree spirit. Her fashion became a reflection of the fun, bold, and unapologetic energy that infused her music.

Katy's fashion choices took center stage with the release of her album, "Teenage Dream." The album's bright, energetic vibe was mirrored in her clothing, from the bubblegum pink dresses she wore in music videos to the whimsical outfits that matched the playful and youthful tone of her music.

Outfits like her "cupcake" dress, her "California Gurls" beach-inspired outfits, and the neon-themed looks she wore during performances became instantly recognizable symbols of her pop star persona.

These fashion statements weren't just for the red carpet or music videos—they were part of the show, turning her performances into visual spectacles that matched the high-energy, colorful sounds of her music.

As Katy's career evolved, so did her fashion. Each album era brought a new look, showcasing her ability to reinvent herself while staying true to her playful, bold essence.

During the *Prism* era, she embraced a more ethereal, goddess-like look, wearing metallics and dreamy, celestial-inspired outfits that reflected the themes of self-discovery and empowerment in her music.

By the time she reached the *Witness* era, Katy's fashion became even more daring, with avant-garde designs and unexpected looks that pushed the boundaries of pop fashion. Through it all, fashion became a tool for telling her story—highlighting her evolution as an artist and woman.

Fashion became a central part of her brand because it was inseparable from her music. Katy's outfits, like her music, made people smile, think, and feel free to express themselves.

Through her ever-changing styles, she showed that fashion is not just about looking good but about embracing individuality, creativity, and fun. By turning fashion into an art form, Katy Perry created a persona that was uniquely hers—a vibrant, fun-loving pop star who isn't afraid to break the rules and have fun along the way.

In this way, fashion became a part of Katy Perry's story, giving fans not just the music they loved but a visual experience that allowed them to connect with her on an even deeper level.

Every outfit told a story, every wig and accessory added another layer to her persona, and together they created a multi-dimensional image that was unforgettable. Katy's fashion became a language all its own, speaking directly to her fans and helping define her place in pop culture history.

CHAPTER 6: KATY PERRY: A VOICE FOR CHANGE

Katy Perry has always used her platform to speak up for causes that are close to her heart. Beyond her catchy pop songs and vibrant personality, she is a passionate advocate for social change, equality, and empowerment.

Whether through her music, public appearances, or activism, Katy Perry has consistently used her voice to inspire others and encourage positive change in the world.

One of the key ways Katy has used her voice for change is through her music. Songs like "Firework" and *"Roar"* became anthems of empowerment, encouraging listeners to embrace their inner strength and never give up.

These songs, with their powerful lyrics and uplifting messages, remind people that they are capable of achieving outstanding things, no matter what challenges they face. "Firework," in particular, became a global anthem of self-acceptance and personal growth, inspiring millions of people to shine brightly and embrace who they are.

Katy's activism extends beyond her music as well. She has long been a supporter of LGBTQ+ rights, using her platform to advocate for acceptance and equality. In 2017, she performed at the "One Love Manchester" benefit concert to honor the victims of the tragic bombing at an Ariana Grande concert.

Her support for LGBTQ+ communities is especially personal to her, as her own journey of self-expression and acceptance has been influenced by her experiences as an ally to those who have often been marginalized.

In addition to advocating for LGBTQ+ rights, Katy is an outspoken supporter of women's rights. She has used her fame to speak out about issues like gender equality, reproductive rights, and the importance of women lifting each other up.

She has also worked with organizations like UNICEF, using her fame to raise awareness for children's rights, education, and health.

Katy Perry's philanthropic efforts are a testament to her belief in using fame for good. She has contributed to many charity events, launched her own initiatives, and supported causes that aim to make the world a better place.

She once said, "I want to be a voice for the voiceless," and that's exactly what she's done, using her influence to make a positive impact on the world.

Katy's dedication to change has also been reflected in her personal growth. Over the years, she has shared her own struggles with mental health, self-doubt, and finding inner peace.

By being open and vulnerable about her own challenges, she has shown fans that it's okay to ask for help and that taking care of your mental and emotional health is just as important as physical well-being.

Through her music, activism, and personal journey, Katy Perry has become more than just a pop star—she has become a voice for change, advocating for equality, empowerment, and social justice.

She continues to inspire millions of fans to speak up, stand up for what they believe in, and make a difference in the world, proving that one person really can create a ripple effect of positive change.

6.1 Songs That Inspire

Katy Perry has always been known for creating music that not only entertains but also inspires. Many of her songs carry powerful messages that encourage people to be brave, confident, and true to themselves.

Her ability to connect with her fans through these uplifting anthems has made her one of the most influential pop stars of her generation.

One of her most iconic songs, "Firework," is a perfect example of how her music can inspire. With lyrics like, "Baby, you're a firework. Come on, show 'em what you're worth," the song encourages listeners to embrace their uniqueness and celebrate who they are. It's a song about overcoming self-doubt and shining brightly, no matter what challenges life may bring.

Another empowering anthem, "Roar," became an anthem of self-empowerment and strength. The song's upbeat tone and bold lyrics encourage listeners to find their voice and stand up for themselves, sending a powerful message of confidence and resilience.

Katy Perry's music has always been about embracing one's inner strength and reminding her fans that they are empowered to make a difference in their own lives and the world around them.

Songs like "Unconditionally" and "Rise" further cement Katy's legacy as a pop star with a purpose. "Unconditionally" is about love and acceptance, not only for others but also for oneself. "Rise" is a call to action, urging people to keep fighting and never give up, no matter how difficult life may be. Katy's music has become a soundtrack for empowerment and personal growth, inspiring millions of people to live authentically and pursue their dreams.

Supporting Important Causes:

Katy Perry has used her fame and platform to support a wide range of causes that are important to her. She believes in using her influence to bring about positive change in the world and has been a vocal advocate for social, environmental, and humanitarian causes throughout her career.

One of the causes Katy is most passionate about is LGBTQ+ rights. As a strong ally to the LGBTQ+ community, she has used her platform to advocate for equal rights and acceptance. In 2017, Katy performed at the "One Love Manchester" benefit concert, which raised funds for victims of a tragic bombing.

Her song "I Kissed a Girl" became an anthem for self-expression, and she has continued to advocate for LGBTQ+ rights in her music and activism.

Katy has also been involved in numerous charity events and has donated her time and money to causes such as children's health, education, and disaster relief. She has partnered with organizations like UNICEF, advocating for children's rights to education, healthcare, and protection.

Her commitment to giving back and supporting vulnerable communities has made her a role model for her fans and a powerful force for positive change in the world.

In addition to her work with children's charities, Katy has been an outspoken advocate for climate change awareness and environmental protection.

She has worked with organizations to raise awareness about the importance of protecting the planet for future generations and has used her social media presence to encourage her fans to take action in their own lives.

Standing Up for What She Believes In:

Katy Perry biography

Kate Perry has never been afraid to stand up for her beliefs, even when they're unpopular. Throughout her career, she has used her voice to speak out on important social and political issues, advocating for change and encouraging her fans to do the same.

One of the most notable ways Katy has stood up for what she believes in is through her advocacy for gender equality. She has used her platform to speak out about the importance of empowering women and fighting for equal rights in all areas of life.

As a successful female artist in the entertainment industry, Katy has been vocal about the challenges women face and has worked to inspire other women to pursue their dreams without fear of judgment.

Katy has also used her voice to support various political causes, particularly when it comes to issues of social justice, LGBTQ+ rights, and human rights.

She has participated in campaigns encouraging people to vote, spoken out in support of marriage equality, and supported initiatives that promote inclusion and diversity. Her activism goes beyond words—she actively participates in efforts to make a real impact in her community and the world.

Additionally, Katy has been open about her personal struggles, including her journey to self-acceptance and mental health challenges.

By sharing her story and advocating for mental health awareness, she has shown that even the most successful people face obstacles and that it's important to seek help when needed. Her openness has inspired countless fans to feel less alone in their own struggles and to prioritize their emotional well-being.

Katy Perry's unwavering commitment to standing up for what she believes in has made her more than just a pop star—she's become a powerful advocate for change, inspiring millions of fans around the world to speak out, get involved, and make a difference in their communities.

Whether through her music, activism, or personal experiences, Katy continues to lead by example, proving that one person truly can make an impact.

CHAPTER 7: THE WORLD OF KATY PERRY'S MUSIC VIDEOS

Katy Perry's music videos are as colorful, creative, and unforgettable as her songs. Known for their whimsical, bold, and sometimes even surreal visuals, her music videos have become an essential part of her identity as an artist.

Each video tells a story, often filled with imaginative characters, vibrant sets, and playful themes, turning her music into an immersive experience that connects with her fans on a deeper level.

From the very beginning of her career, Katy's music videos have been an extension of her artistic vision, combining elements of fantasy, humor, and fantasy-like settings. One of her earliest and most iconic videos, "I Kissed a Girl,"* introduced the world to Katy's quirky, fun-loving style.

The video featured a playful, carefree atmosphere with bold, colorful visuals that matched the song's cheeky lyrics. This playful aesthetic would become a hallmark of her music videos throughout her career.

As Katy's career evolved, so did the ambition of her music videos. "Teenage Dream" (the video) took viewers on a dreamy, nostalgic journey, capturing the carefree, summer-loving spirit of youth.

The visuals were as sweet and vibrant as the song itself, with scenes set in a colorful world that felt like a never-ending summer. This video, like many others in Katy's repertoire, invited fans to escape reality and step into a world filled with vibrant hues and fantastical themes.

"Firework" is another music video that left a lasting impression. The video, with its stunning visuals of people overcoming their struggles and finding empowerment, matched the song's message of self-acceptance and embracing one's inner strength.

It was not just a visual masterpiece but also a motivational experience, encouraging viewers to embrace their uniqueness and shine brightly. The use of fireworks as a metaphor for personal growth and freedom was a powerful visual element that became iconic in its own right.

In "E.T."* (featuring Kanye West), Katy's music video took fans into a futuristic world, blending sci-fi with her love of fantasy. With her alien-inspired makeup and costumes, Katy's character transforms into a cosmic, otherworldly figure, echoing the song's themes of alien love and escape from the ordinary.

The video's special effects, including space landscapes and surreal imagery, gave fans a glimpse of Katy's ability to create a narrative through stunning, high-concept visuals.

Perhaps one of her most playful and imaginative videos came with "California Gurls." The video felt like a candy-colored dreamland with scenes of beaches made of cotton candy, a giant ice cream cone, and even a water fight with beach balls. Everything about this video screamed summer fun, vibrant color, and playful adventure, reinforcing the song's carefree attitude and bright, sunny energy.

Katy Perry's videos often play with themes of self-expression, empowerment, and boldness. Whether she's dressed as a candy princess or a glamorous diva, her music videos allow her to bring her creative visions to life in ways that captivate and inspire her audience.

Beyond just promoting songs, Katy's music videos are an art form in themselves, showcasing her love for storytelling, fantasy, and fun.

Through her music videos, Katy Perry has redefined what it means to combine music with visuals. She's used these videos to create a universe all her own—one filled with color, creativity, and a sense of wonder.

From "Roar" to "Dark Horse," each video continues to show her willingness to push boundaries, experiment with new ideas, and immerse her fans in her world of vibrant imagination. As much as her music speaks to the heart, her videos speak to the eyes, making the whole Katy Perry experience unforgettable.

7.1 Creating Visual Masterpieces

Katy Perry's music videos are not just extensions of her songs; they are visual masterpieces that captivate and transport audiences into colorful, dream-like worlds. From the very start of her career, Katy understood that music and visuals could work together to create something even more magical.

Her videos have become as iconic as her songs, with vibrant sets, dazzling costumes, and imaginative concepts that push the limits of what pop music videos can be.

One of the key elements of Katy's visual storytelling is her attention to detail. Every music video feels like a carefully crafted world where every color, prop, and design serves a purpose.

Whether it's the candy-coated dreamland in *"California Gurls"* or the futuristic, alien-inspired world of *"E.T."*Katy's videos are known for their bold visual choices that bring her creative vision to life. Each video is a carefully thought-out production, where every frame feels like a work of art.

In videos like "Teenage Dream" and "Last Friday Night (T.G.I.F.)*,* Katy captures the carefree, youthful spirit with playful sets, bright colors, and whimsical touches that draw the viewer into the narrative. These visual masterpieces are often filled with humor, fantasy, and personal expression, allowing Katy to connect with her audience in a way that only a visual medium can.

The Magic Behind the Videos

Behind every unforgettable Katy Perry music video is a team of talented creators who bring her wild ideas to life. The magic behind her videos comes from the collaboration of visionary directors, creative designers, makeup artists, and special effects teams who help turn her imaginative concepts into reality.

Katy herself is deeply involved in the creative process of her videos. Known for her bold fashion choices and larger-than-life persona, she often works closely with directors to ensure that her music videos reflect her personal style and artistic vision.

Her willingness to experiment and push boundaries is what makes her videos stand out from other artists. Whether it's a colorful, over-the-top scene or a stunning, cinematic visual, Katy's input plays a vital role in making each video truly unique.

For instance, the "Roar" video was directed by Grady Hall and features stunning jungle landscapes, vibrant animal-inspired outfits, and visuals that emphasize self-empowerment and independence.

The magical blend of exotic visuals with Katy's fearless performance shows just how much attention goes into the creation of each scene. Special effects, elaborate sets, and skilled choreography all combine to create the illusion of a powerful adventure that matches the strength of the song itself.

The creative magic behind "Dark Horse," with its ancient Egyptian theme and larger-than-life set designs, showcased Katy's love for mythology and dramatic visuals. It was one of her most extravagant music videos, with intricate costumes and spectacular effects that helped bring the song's futuristic yet mystical atmosphere to life.

The magic behind these visuals is not just in the extravagant sets, but in how they mirror the themes of her songs and amplify the emotional connection with her audience.

Unforgettable Moments from "Firework" and "Roar":
Both "Firework" and "Roar" stand out as two of Katy Perry's most unforgettable music videos, not only for their visual creativity but also for the powerful messages they convey.

In "Firework," one of the most memorable moments is when Katy Perry herself is standing in front of a fireworks display, symbolizing how people can overcome their inner struggles and shine bright despite challenges.

The video is filled with emotional moments, showing people from all walks of life facing personal battles and finding strength within themselves. The imagery of fireworks bursting into the sky, set against beautiful backdrops, perfectly captures the essence of the song—encouraging people to embrace their inner "firework" and let their light shine.

In "Roar," one of the most unforgettable moments is when Katy emerges from a jungle, roaring like a lioness, dressed in a fierce outfit, and standing tall against her obstacles. The video shows Katy transforming into a jungle queen, confronting her fears and finding the strength to stand up for herself.

The stunning visuals of wild animals, lush jungles, and a powerful, confident Katy Perry make this video a celebration of empowerment and resilience. The symbolism of her taking charge of her life, standing up to her challenges, and roaring triumphantly resonated with millions of viewers.

Both videos are filled with dramatic visuals that perfectly complement the themes of their songs. Whether it's the inspiring message of self-empowerment in *"Firework"* or the fearless attitude of *"Roar," these music videos are unforgettable because they connect deeply with the emotions of the audience.

They remind viewers that no matter what struggles they may face, they have the power within themselves to rise above and shine brightly. Katy Perry's "Firework" and "Roar" videos remain timeless classics, inspiring millions of fans around the world to embrace their own strength and confidence.

CHAPTER 8: CHALLENGES AND TRIUMPHS

Katy Perry's journey to superstardom has been filled with both challenges and triumphs, each shaping her into the resilient and inspiring artist she is today. Like many successful figures, her path to fame wasn't always easy, but her determination, creativity, and ability to overcome obstacles have been key to her success. Through every setback, Katy found a way to rise stronger, more determined, and ready to face whatever came next.

Challenges Along the Way:

Before Katy Perry became the global pop sensation we know today, she faced numerous challenges that tested her resolve. One of the biggest hurdles early in her career was finding her voice and establishing a unique musical identity.

After initially trying her hand at Christian music, Katy struggled to break through in the mainstream music industry. Her early attempts were met with rejection, and she faced many "no's" before she found the right opportunity.

Her breakthrough came with the release of "I Kissed a Girl," but even then, the song was controversial. The subject matter sparked discussions and debates, with some questioning her motives and others criticizing the song for its boldness.

Katy faced criticism for pushing boundaries and defying social norms, but she stuck to her artistic vision and continued to create music that reflected her true self.

Another challenge Katy has faced is the pressure that comes with being a public figure. The constant scrutiny from the media and fans can be overwhelming, especially when it comes to her personal life.

Katy's relationships and personal experiences have been frequently discussed in the press, and while she's openly shared her journey, the constant attention can be difficult to navigate. In spite of this, Katy has remained focused on her career and has used her experiences to fuel her creativity.

Additionally, Katy has spoken openly about the mental health struggles she has faced, including battles with anxiety and depression. In 2020, she revealed in an interview that she had considered taking a break from music after a tough period in her life.

However, she realized that she needed to confront these challenges head-on and used the time to focus on self-care and healing. Her vulnerability has resonated with her fans, making her a role model for others going through similar struggles.

Triumphs and Achievements:

Katy Perry's triumphs are a testament to her perseverance and creative spirit. After overcoming early setbacks, her music finally took off with the release of "One of the Boys" and the breakthrough single "I Kissed a Girl." The song not only topped charts worldwide but also propelled Katy into the spotlight as a bold new voice in pop music.

Her biggest triumph came with the release of her second album, "Teenage Dream." With massive hits like "California Gurls," "Teenage Dream," and

"Firework," The album cemented her place in pop music history.

"Teenage Dream" became one of the best-selling albums of the decade, and Katy became the first woman to have five number-one singles from one album on the Billboard Hot 100. This achievement solidified her as a global superstar and a force to be reckoned with in the music industry.

Beyond chart-topping hits, Katy's triumphs include her ability to connect with her audience on a deep level. Her music videos, live performances, and public persona have allowed her to create a world that fans want to be a part of.

Whether it's the empowering anthem of "Roar" or the heartwarming message in "Firework," Katy's songs inspire millions around the world to believe in themselves, be brave, and follow their dreams.

In addition to her musical achievements, Katy Perry has successfully ventured into other areas, including acting, television, and philanthropy. She has appeared as a judge on *American Idol*, where her down-to-earth personality and willingness to mentor young artists have made her a beloved figure.

Katy has also used her platform to support important causes, from LGBTQ+ rights to children's health, demonstrating that her influence extends beyond music.

Katy's personal life also saw major milestones, including her marriage to actor Orlando Bloom and the birth of their daughter, Daisy Dove.

These life changes have been celebrated by her fans, showing that despite the challenges, Katy has been able to find happiness and fulfillment outside of her career.

Overcoming Obstacles and Rising Stronger

Katy Perry's career is defined by her ability to overcome obstacles and use those experiences to fuel her creative output. Whether it's dealing with rejection, navigating public scrutiny, or battling personal struggles, Katy has shown that challenges are an inevitable part of success—but they don't define her. Her triumphs are a result of her refusal to give up, her dedication to her craft, and her ability to turn adversity into opportunity.

Through it all, Katy Perry has remained a symbol of resilience and hope. Her journey proves that even in the face of setbacks, it's possible to rise, evolve, and achieve greatness.

As she continues to inspire with her music and activism, Katy Perry's story is a reminder that every challenge faced can lead to a triumph that is even greater than imagined.

8.1 How Katy Perry Stayed True to Herself

Katy Perry's success can be attributed not only to her immense talent but also to her unwavering commitment to staying true to herself. Throughout her career, she has never been afraid to embrace her individuality, express her unique artistic vision, and challenge expectations, both in her music and in her personal life.

In a world where pop stars often face immense pressure to conform to trends, Katy has remained authentic, using her platform to celebrate her quirks and passions.

From the very beginning of her career, Katy made the conscious decision to follow her own path. After initially attempting to break into the Christian music scene, she realized that her true calling was in pop music, where she could express herself fully and without restrictions.

With boldness and confidence, she reinvented herself with the release of "I Kissed a Girl," a song that was not only a commercial hit but also a statement of her individuality. Katy didn't let outside voices dictate her direction; instead, she chose to make the kind of music that felt true to her, regardless of what was expected.

One of the defining aspects of Katy's career has been her refusal to shy away from being a colorful, larger-than-life version of herself. Her love for bold fashion, vibrant colors, and whimsical, imaginative visuals has become a signature part of her brand.

She often uses her music videos, performances, and public appearances to express her creative freedom and push the boundaries of traditional pop culture.

Whether she's dressed as a candy princess in *"California Gurls"* or embodying a fierce jungle queen in "Roar," Katy stays true to her vision of making music that is fun, empowering, and unapologetically herself.

Katy's authenticity extends beyond her artistry into her personal beliefs and values. She has been outspoken about causes she believes in, such as LGBTQ+ rights, mental health awareness, and gender equality, using her fame as a platform to advocate for change.

She has also been open about her struggles, including her mental health challenges and personal setbacks, which has allowed her fans to connect with her on a deeper, more human level. By sharing her vulnerabilities, Katy has shown that it's okay to embrace imperfections and that being real with yourself and others is a powerful form of strength.

Moreover, Katy has never been afraid to take risks and experiment with her sound and style. She has constantly evolved as an artist, from the rebellious pop anthems of "One of the Boys" to the more introspective and empowering messages of "Witness." She continually reinvents herself, yet always remains grounded in the core of who she is—a bold, creative, and fearless individual.

Throughout her career, Katy Perry's commitment to staying true to herself has made her not only a successful artist but also an inspiration to millions.

She proves that being yourself is the most powerful thing you can do by navigating fame to stay authentic.

Whether she's singing about love, self-empowerment, or social justice, Katy has built a legacy by following her heart and staying true to her unique voice in both music and life.

CHAPTER 9: JUDGE ON AMERICAN IDOL

As part of the judging panel, alongside fellow judges Lionel Richie and Luke Bryan, Katy brought her unique blend of humor, compassion, and candidness to the show, quickly becoming a fan favorite.

Her approach to judging was always warm and constructive. She offered insightful feedback to contestants, balancing honesty with encouragement. Katy understood that the journey to stardom can be difficult, and she often focused on helping contestants find their authentic selves, just as she had done throughout her career.

Instead of simply critiquing performances, Katy encouraged contestants to embrace their individuality and to connect emotionally with their music. She would often share her own experiences and lessons learned, making the feedback more personal and relatable.

Katy's sense of humor also shone through on the panel. Known for her playful and larger-than-life persona, she brought lightheartedness and fun to the show. She wasn't afraid to make jokes, be goofy, or even have a little fun with her fellow judges, creating an atmosphere that was both entertaining and inviting for both the contestants and the viewers.

Katy's candid and approachable style made her a standout on the show, and she quickly became known for her lively and sometimes unpredictable comments, which kept the audience engaged.

One of the most impactful parts of Katy's judging role was her genuine investment in the contestants' success. She took the time to get to know each contestant, offering not just professional advice but also emotional support.

Her emotional reactions to powerful performances, whether it was crying over a heartfelt song or getting excited over an impressive vocal performance, showed viewers how much she cared about the journey of each contestant. Katy was more than just a judge—she became a mentor, rooting for contestants to grow and succeed.

Katy's time on *American Idol* allowed her to connect with a new generation of aspiring artists, giving them the opportunity to showcase their talents on a massive platform. Her involvement in the show reinforced her reputation as an artist who values creativity, authenticity, and hard work.

By offering a blend of practical advice and emotional encouragement, Katy Perry helped shape the careers of countless young singers, and her time on *American Idol* further solidified her place as an influential figure in the music industry.

9.1 Bringing Fun and Kindness to the Show

Katy Perry brought a unique energy to *American Idol*, combining her vibrant personality with a deep sense of kindness that set her apart as a judge. Her playful sense of humor and approachable demeanor created a welcoming atmosphere, making contestants feel at ease even in high-pressure moments.

Katy often used her natural charisma to lighten the mood, whether by cracking a joke, giving a quirky compliment, or playfully bantering with her fellow judges. These moments of levity not only entertained viewers but also helped contestants relax and perform at their best.

Kindness was at the heart of Katy's approach to judging. She always ensured her feedback was constructive and uplifting, even when pointing out areas for improvement.

Rather than focusing solely on technical flaws, she emphasized the importance of authenticity and personal growth, encouraging contestants to embrace their individuality.

Katy's empathy shone through when contestants shared emotional backstories or struggled with self-confidence. She consistently offered words of encouragement, reminding them of their potential and inspiring them to keep pushing forward.

Mentoring the Next Generation of Stars:

As a judge, Katy took on the role of mentor with enthusiasm, sharing her wealth of experience in the music industry to guide aspiring artists. She understood the challenges of breaking into the industry and used her platform to help contestants navigate those hurdles.

Her advice was often rooted in her own journey—she openly shared stories of her struggles, setbacks, and triumphs to motivate and connect with the contestants.

Katy's mentorship extended beyond technical critiques. She encouraged contestants to think about their artistry holistically, advising them on everything from stage presence to song selection.

She emphasized the importance of storytelling through music, urging contestants to connect emotionally with their performances and audiences. Katy often helped contestants find their unique voices, reinforcing the idea that individuality and authenticity are key to standing out in a competitive industry.

She also supported contestants on a personal level, addressing issues like stagefright, self-doubt, and resilience. Her candid discussions about mental health and the pressures of fame made her relatable and approachable. By creating a safe space for contestants to express themselves, Katy helped them grow not only as artists but also as individuals.

Her Impact Beyond the Stage:

Katy Perry biography

Katy Perry's influence on *American Idol* extended far beyond the confines of the show. Her presence as a judge brought fresh perspectives and reinforced important messages about kindness, resilience, and staying true to oneself. By sharing her personal experiences and advocating for authenticity, she inspired not just the contestants but also the millions of viewers who tuned in each week.

Katy used her platform to champion diversity and inclusivity in the music industry. She celebrated contestants' unique backgrounds and encouraged them to embrace their cultural identities, proving that music has the power to unite and inspire.

Her support of social causes, such as mental health awareness and LGBTQ+ rights, further demonstrated her commitment to making a positive impact beyond her music career.

Her role on the show also highlighted the importance of mentorship. Katy's guidance gave contestants the tools they needed to succeed, instilling in them the confidence to pursue their dreams. Many former contestants have spoken about how her advice and encouragement helped shape their careers, showing the lasting effect of her mentorship.

Katy Perry's time on *American Idol* wasn't just about discovering new talent—it was about fostering a culture of kindness, empowerment, and creativity.

Her ability to connect with people on a personal level, combined with her wealth of experience and unshakable optimism, made her a standout judge and a lasting influence on the show and its contestants.

Through her efforts, Katy proved that being a successful artist is not just about talent—it's about staying true to yourself, lifting others up, and using your platform to inspire positive change.

CHAPTER 10: PERSONAL LIFE

Katy Perry's personal life is as vibrant and inspiring as her music career. Born as Katheryn Elizabeth Hudson on October 25, 1984, in Santa Barbara, California, Katy grew up in a deeply religious household. Her parents, Keith and Mary Hudson, were Pentecostal ministers, and her early life was shaped by a strict Christian upbringing. Despite this, Katy's creative spirit shone through, and her passion for music became her calling.

Over the years, Katy's personal journey has been marked by moments of joy, growth, and challenges that have shaped her into the dynamic individual she is today. While her professional life has been filled with massive success, her personal life has seen its own ups and downs, showcasing her resilience and strength.

Family and Relationships:

Katy is currently in a relationship with actor Orlando Bloom. The couple began dating in 2016, and after a brief split, they reunited and became engaged in 2019.

Their relationship is often described as playful and supportive, with both being deeply committed to each other and their shared family goals. In August 2020, Katy and Orlando welcomed their daughter, Daisy Dove Bloom.

Katy has often spoken about how motherhood has transformed her life, describing Daisy as her greatest gift and a source of unconditional love.

In interviews, Katy has shared how becoming a mother has given her a new perspective on life and helped her find balance between her personal and professional worlds. She embraces the challenges of parenting and often expresses her gratitude for the joy that Daisy has brought into her life.

Faith and Spirituality:

While Katy moved away from the strict religious beliefs of her childhood, her faith and spirituality remain important aspects of her life.

She has spoken about her ongoing journey to reconcile her past with her present, finding ways to embrace both her upbringing and her current beliefs. Katy often reflects on the values instilled in her by her parents, such as compassion and gratitude, which continue to guide her today.

Mental health and self-care.

Katy has been open about her struggles with mental health, particularly during challenging periods in her career and personal life.

She has candidly shared her experiences with anxiety and depression, especially during moments when she felt disconnected from her identity or purpose. Her honesty has resonated with fans, inspiring many to seek help and prioritize their own mental well-being.

For Katy, self-care is an essential part of maintaining balance. She practices meditation and yoga, which help her stay grounded amidst the demands of her career. She also emphasizes the importance of therapy and self-reflection in her journey toward healing and personal growth.

Friendships and Hobbies:

Katy values her close friendships and often surrounds herself with a tight-knit group of supportive people. Despite her busy schedule, she makes time for her loved ones and cherishes moments of laughter and connection.

In her downtime, Katy enjoys hobbies like painting, hiking, and spending time with her family. She also has a love for traveling and exploring new cultures, which she often incorporates into her creative process.

Philanthropy and Giving Back:

Katy's personal life is deeply intertwined with her commitment to giving back. She is actively involved in charitable work, supporting causes such as children's education, disaster relief, and LGBTQ+ rights.

Katy serves as a UNICEF Goodwill Ambassador, using her platform to raise awareness about global issues and make a positive impact on the world.

Katy Perry's personal life is a testament to her authenticity, resilience, and compassion. Whether she's navigating motherhood, giving back to her community, or focusing on her own mental health, Katy continues to inspire others with her openness and strength.

She proves that even amidst the spotlight, it's possible to remain grounded, embrace challenges, and find joy in life's simplest moments.

10.1 Katy Perry as a Mom and Partner

Katy Perry's life as a mom and partner has added a deeply personal and rewarding layer to her already extraordinary journey. With her fiancé, actor Orlando Bloom, and their daughter, Daisy Dove Bloom, Katy has embraced family life with the same passion and energy she brings to her career.

Her role as a mother and partner reveals a softer, more grounded side of the pop superstar, showing her ability to balance her demanding career with the joys and challenges of family life.

Balancing Fame with Family:

For Katy, balancing her global fame with her role as a mother has been both transformational and fulfilling. Since welcoming Daisy in August 2020, Katy has often described motherhood as her greatest and most humbling accomplishment.

She speaks openly about how becoming a mom has given her a new perspective on life, helping her prioritize what truly matters and embrace a slower, more intentional pace.

Despite her busy schedule as an artist and television judge, Katy is deeply committed to being present for her daughter. She often shares how she and Orlando work as a team to ensure Daisy feels supported and loved, even amidst their hectic careers.

Whether it's making time for family vacations or incorporating Daisy into her daily routine, Katy emphasizes the importance of quality time and creating cherished memories.

Katy's dedication to her family doesn't mean she's given up on her career—quite the opposite. She's found ways to integrate both worlds, proving that it's possible to have a thriving career while being a hands-on parent.

Katy has said that motherhood has enhanced her creativity and given her a renewed sense of purpose, fueling her drive to create music and art that reflects her evolving identity.

How She Inspires Others to Dream Big:

Katy Perry's journey as a mom and partner is a powerful example of how dreams can evolve without losing their magic.

She's candid about the challenges of balancing fame, family, and personal growth, but she consistently emphasizes the importance of following your passions while staying true to yourself.

By showing that she can pursue her career and be a devoted mother, Katy inspires others to believe that they don't have to choose between their dreams and their personal lives.

Katy also uses her platform to encourage other women to embrace their multifaceted identities. Whether she's speaking about the joys of motherhood or the lessons she's learned as a partner, Katy offers a relatable and empowering message: it's okay to be vulnerable, to ask for help, and to grow in every stage of life.

She reminds her fans that life is about balance, resilience, and the courage to keep dreaming, no matter the circumstances.

Her relationship with Orlando Bloom is another source of inspiration.

Their partnership is built on mutual respect, support, and a shared commitment to family. Katy often describes their dynamic as playful yet deeply rooted in love and understanding.

The couple's journey—from falling in love to overcoming challenges and celebrating their shared milestones—demonstrates the beauty of partnership and the importance of nurturing each other's individuality.

CHAPTER 11: LEGACY

As Katy Perry continues to balance her life as a global superstar with her roles as a mom and partner, she sets an example of how success and personal fulfillment can coexist. Her ability to navigate the complexities of fame while remaining authentic and family-focused serves as a beacon of hope for others striving to achieve their dreams.

Through her honesty, vulnerability, and determination, Katy shows that even the brightest stars have room to grow, evolve, and find deeper meaning in their lives. Whether through her music, her family life, or her advocacy for self-expression, Katy Perry inspires millions to dream big, embrace change, and create their own definitions of happiness and success.

Katy Perry's legacy is as vibrant and unforgettable as the career she has built over the years. From her bold beginnings as a small-town girl with big dreams to becoming one of the most iconic and influential pop stars of her generation, Katy's story is a testament to resilience, creativity, and authenticity. She has left an indelible mark on the music industry, not only with her chart-topping hits but also with her unapologetic embrace of individuality and self-expression.

Katy's music is her most powerful legacy. Songs like "Firework," "Roar," and "Teenage Dream" have become anthems for self-confidence, empowerment, and joy.

Her ability to craft relatable lyrics paired with infectious melodies has made her a voice for people of all ages, encouraging them to embrace who they are and chase their dreams. These songs aren't just hits—they're celebrations of life, and they've inspired millions around the world to believe in their own potential.

But Katy's impact goes beyond her music. Her fearless approach to fashion and performance has redefined what it means to be a pop star.

She has consistently pushed boundaries with her elaborate costumes, daring music videos, and spectacular live shows, all of which showcase her boundless creativity. Katy's colorful and playful aesthetic has made her a cultural icon, proving that art can be as fun as it is meaningful.

As a role model, Katy has used her platform to advocate for important causes, from mental health awareness to LGBTQ+ rights. Her philanthropic efforts, including her work as a UNICEF Goodwill

Ambassador, highlight her dedication to making the world a better place.

By speaking openly about her own challenges and successes, Katy has shown that even those who seem larger than life are human, relatable, and capable of great kindness.

Katy's legacy also lives on through her role as a mother and mentor. Her journey into motherhood has added a deeply personal dimension to her life, and she has shared how her daughter, Daisy, inspires her to be the best version of herself. On shows like *American Idol,* Katy has helped nurture the next generation of artists, passing on the lessons she's learned and encouraging others to find their unique voices.

Ultimately, Katy Perry's legacy is one of color, creativity, and courage. She has shown that it's okay to dream big, be bold, and embrace your whole self. Whether through her music, her philanthropy, or her personal story, Katy has created a legacy that will continue to inspire people for generations to come.

With every note she sings and every stage she graces, Katy reminds us all that life is meant to be lived boldly, joyfully, and in full, vibrant color.

CONCLUSION

Katy Perry's journey from a small-town girl with big dreams to a world-famous pop queen shows us that anything is possible when you believe in yourself.

She didn't give up, even when people told her no or when things got tough. Instead, she worked hard, stayed true to her unique style, and kept chasing her dreams.

Her songs remind us to be confident, express ourselves, and never stop dreaming. Whether she's singing about being a firework or standing up for what's right, Katy teaches us that we all have a special light inside—we just have to let it shine.

So remember: if Katy Perry can turn her teenage dream into a reality, so can you. Keep dreaming big, stay creative, and always be proud of who you are. The world is waiting for your spark.

Made in United States
Troutdale, OR
04/20/2025

30756923R00064